**At Issue**

The Olympics

# Other Books in the At Issue Series:

# At Issue

## The Olympics

*Noah Berlatsky, Book Editor*

**GREENHAVEN PRESS**
*A part of Gale, Cengage Learning*

GALE
CENGAGE Learning·

Farmington Hills, Mich • San Francisco • New York • Waterville, Maine
Meriden, Conn • Mason, Ohio • Chicago

Judy Galens, *Manager, Frontlist Acquisitions*

*For more information, contact:*
Greenhaven Press
27500 Drake Rd.
Farmington Hills, MI 48331-3535
Or you can visit our Internet site at gale.cengage.com

For product information and technology assistance, contact us at

Gale Customer Support, 1-800-877-4253
For permission to use material from this text or product, submit all requests online at www.cengage.com/permissions

Further permissions questions can be e-mailed to permissionrequest@cengage.com

Articles in Greenhaven Press anthologies are often edited for length to meet page requirements. In addition, original titles of these works are changed to clearly present the main thesis and to explicitly indicate the author's opinion. Every effort is made to ensure that Greenhaven Press accurately reflects the original intent of the authors. Every effort has been made to trace the owners of copyrighted material.

Cover image © GStar.

**LIBRARY OF CONGRESS CATALOGING-IN-PUBLICATION DATA**

The Olympics / Noah Berlatsky, Book Editor.
    pages cm. -- (At issue)
Includes bibliographical references and index.
ISBN 978-0-7377-7398-9 (hardcover) -- ISBN 978-0-7377-7399-6 (paperback)
1. Olympics. I. Berlatsky, Noah.
GV721.5.O39275 2016
796.48--dc23
                            2015026887

Printed in the United States of America
1 2 3 4 5       20 19 18 17 16

# Contents

# Introduction

The Paralympic Games are an international sports competition for athletes with physical disabilities such as paraplegia or quadriplegia, amputation, vision impairment, small stature, and other similar disabilities. The Paralympic Games are separate from the Special Olympics, which are for athletes with mental or developmental disabilities.

The Paralympic Games originated at the 1948 Olympics in London, when sixteen injured veterans in wheelchairs took part in an archery competition. Known as the Stoke Mandeville Games, the contest officially became the Paralympics in Rome in 1960, when four hundred athletes from twenty-three countries competed. The games were then held every four years. In 1976, the first Winter Paralympics were held. Beginning in 1988, the Paralympic Games have been held immediately after the Summer and Winter Olympics.

The Paralympic Games have achieved a great degree of visibility in recent years because of South African sprint runner Oscar Pistorius, both of whose legs are amputated below the knee. Pistorius was a paralympic champion who then sought to enter able-bodied events. Despite objections by sports administrative organizations, which argued that Pistorius's artificial limbs gave him an unfair advantage, he was finally allowed to run in the 2012 Summer Olympics, where he won gold in the 400-metre race and the 4x400 metres relay race. His success brought unprecedented attention to disabled athletes.

Perhaps in part because of Pistorius's success, the Paralympics have become a source of some controversy. Those who support the games see it as an opportunity to highlight the accomplishments of the disabled and to draw needed attention, and perhaps funding, to sports for those with disability. For example, Kath Vickery, a woman who is blind, was quoted at the BBC expressing enthusiasm about the 2012 London Paralympics: "I'm excited because I think the Paralympics could elevate the standing of disability sport in the UK and raise its profile," she said.[1]

Stella Young at ABC in Australia also argues that the Paralympics is important for people with disabilities. "When we hear athletes say there's nothing like the Paralympics, they don't just mean the competition,"[2] Young says. She added:

Last Tuesday I popped into the athlete's village and what I found absolutely took my breath away. Or, more accurately, I felt a familiar kind of release in my chest, one that I've felt before at disability conferences and events. It can only really be described as the moment you realise you're in an environment where you can truly be yourself; the feeling of being among your people, if you will.[3]

Young states that for someone with disability, the Paralympics is "Acceptance heaven."

Other writers, however, have criticized the Paralympics and argued that they don't advance the cause of disabled people. Daphnee Denis writing for *Slate*, for example, argues that separating the Paralympics and the Olympics makes disabled athletes less visible. She suggests that the two games should be combined into a single Olympics, with some events for the disabled. Denis points to goalball, a sport for visually impaired athletes. Goalball does not receive much attention, because it does not mirror an able-bodied sport. Goalball athletes struggle to fund their training. "To provide them with professional funding," Denis says, "there needs to be an audi-

1. Quoted in Michael Hirst, "London 2012: Paralympics Divide Opinion, Survey Suggests," BBC, December 3, 2011. http://www.bbc.com/news/uk-16004258.
2. Stella Young, "Embrace and Celebrate the Paralympic Spotlight," ABC, September 3, 2012. http://www.abc.net.au/rampup/articles/2012/09/03/3582092.htm.
3. Ibid.

ence for goalball. . . ."[4] A merger with the Olympics proper, she feels, would provide that audience. In a merger, disabled athletes would contribute to their nation's medal count and, "By earning gold for their country, Paralympians would finally be seen for what they really are: true champions."[5]

Robert Jones, writing for *The Guardian*, argues that in many cases the Paralympics does not help disabled people but instead increases the stigma they face. Regular Olympians, he says, are recognized as exceptional. No one expects every able-bodied person they meet on the street to run as fast as Usain Bolt or Florence Griffith Joyner. But, Jones adds, "it's commonplace to hear 'if he can do it so can you' as a rebuke or encouragement to disabled people."[6] This can be especially dangerous, Jones says, when the spectacle of Paralympians is used to suggest that people with disabilities do not need government aid or medical help.

The remainder of *At Issue: The Olympics* examines other controversial issues around the Olympics, including whether the Olympic games benefit host cities, whether the games are environmentally dangerous, whether the Special Olympics benefit people with mental disabilities, and whether doping and steroid use should be allowed in the games. As with the controversy surrounding the Paralympics, these discussions highlight the importance of the Olympics and differing viewpoints on the Olympic spirit.

4. Daphnee Denis, "Scrap the Paralympics," *Slate*, August 9, 2012. http://www.slate.com/ articles/sports/fivering_circus/2012/08/paralympics_2012_it_s_time_to_scrap_the _paralympic_games_disabled_athletes_should_compete_in_the_olympics_too_.html.
5. Ibid.
6. Robert Jones, "Sorry, the Paralympic Spirit Insults Disabled People Like Me," *Guardian*, August 30, 2012. http://www.theguardian.com/commentisfree/2012/aug/30 /paralympic-spirit-insults-disabled-like-me.

# 1

# Vancouver Gained Important Benefits from Hosting the Olympics

*Brent Toderian*

*Brent Toderian is president of TODERIAN UrbanWORKS, a Vancouver-based city planning and urbanism consultancy, and past director of city planning for Vancouver.*

*Hosting the Olympics is a big task. In 2010, when hosting the winter games, Vancouver and its people were concerned that the cost would be too high, and that facilities would not be ready. However, in the end, the games were very successful, showed Vancouver in a good light, and created a great spirit of civic togetherness. The Olympics also led to much sustainable building and public architecture that remained long after the games had gone.*

As billions await the London Olympics' opening ceremonies, global urbanists are already deep into the sport of navel-gazing. Has London mimicked former host Beijing, focusing on national reputation-building and expensive attention-seeking architectural icons? Or have they followed in the carbon-footsteps of Vancouver, the last Winter Games host, with weighty aspirations to use the Olympics as a catalyst for sustainable and inclusive city-building?

## The Vancouver Games

Watching the London Games approach has brought back my own memories of our experiences with the 2010 Vancouver Games. Olympic host cities of all stripes share a rare and special collective memory and experience. The days leading up to the 2010 Games were filled with hand-wringing, anxiousness and criticisms.

From weather fears to concerns that locals wouldn't truly embrace the Games, there was lots to lose sleep over for VANOC [Vancouver Organizing Committee] and its many partners. Indeed, for Vancouver, tangles and tragedy struck early. Who could have predicted warm weather with no snow, a cauldron malfunction during the Opening Ceremonies, and most sadly, a devastating athlete death on the first day? In those first moments, things felt grim.

---

*It might help Londoners to know that there had been plenty of pre-Games grumbling in Vancouver too.*

---

For those of us in city-building the big work of facilities-design was long done, because it had to be, along with developing the Olympics Transportation Plan, and envisioning public space transformations, "look-of-the-city" elements and spectacles. But the logistics of being a good host to thousands of athletes, media and visitors kept everyone tense and hopping.

Like in London, officials were obsessed with Olympics branding issues, with predictable debates about free speech in the public realm. Hundreds of meetings were organized for local and regional economic development, as well as special events hosted with global partners such as the Clinton Climate Initiative and Sir Richard Branson.

A big part of our job during the Games would be as ambassadors to the global media, as well as to political, city-building and economic development delegations intrigued by our preparations (especially our LEED-ND [Leadership in Energy & Environmental Design-Neighborhood Development] Platinum Olympic Athletes Village, dubbed by the U.S. Green Building Council as the "greenest community in North America" at the beginning of the Games). We also kept busy with unexpected challenges, like negotiating an improved redesign of the unfortunate Olympic Cauldron condition, infamously hidden behind harsh chain-link fencing.

## Pre-Game Jitters

It might help Londoners to know that there had been plenty of pre-Games grumbling in Vancouver too. Many pledged to "get out of town during the Games"; others complained "we never should have gone after the Olympics." We, like the rest of the world, had been affected by the global economic crisis in 2008, and debates about whether the Games would help or cost us economically abounded.

I followed with great interest London Mayor Boris Johnson's recent call to grumpy pre-Olympics Londoners to "put a sock in it." Although this is a bit more aggressive language than we Canadians might have used, our own mayor also had to encourage Vancouverites to stay positive in the days leading up to the opening ceremonies. The concept of a "pre-Olympics funk" is well understood by host cities. There was considerable worry that Vancouverites would put on an unhappy face when the visitors arrived and cameras started rolling.

When I was interviewed by Nate Berg in *Places Journal* in 2010, here's how I put it:

> Past Olympic cities have talked about the emotional roller coaster that happens before an Olympics, and sometimes you have to go through the troughs to get to the high points. I think our city has had that. Vancouver is a very self-aware city. We can be tough on ourselves and that's one reason we've achieved as much as we have. But it can be a challenge

to balance between booster-ism and cynicism about our place in the world, and how well we've achieved our goals around the Olympics and around sustainability. But as we get closer and closer to the day, it's just more excitement and less worry. As they say, at this point it's like a luge sled: no brakes and limited steering!

---

*The Olympics can be an incredible city and nation-changing moment—if it's designed that way, and the people embrace it.*

---

## Civic Transformation

As it turned out, organizers needn't have worried. Vancouverites and visitors teamed up to make the 2010 Olympics a new benchmark in Olympics-related civic transformation and celebrations. The public embraced the complete Olympic experience in the city and its streets like never before, fostered by beautiful shorts-weather and a city-led focus on making the Olympic energy accessible to everyone, not just those who had tickets. The whole city was the Olympics, something that changed us as a city forever, and changed the Country and the Olympics as well.

Vancouver's Games will be remembered not for our gold medals, though that final gold in hockey, defeating the U.S. in overtime, has become part of Canada's collective cultural memory. It will be remembered not for the things that were out of the host city's control, the mechanical glitches or the initial media snickers. It will be remembered for how the organizers responded and recovered, and how the city celebrated. It will be remembered for perhaps the strongest effect on national unity, identity and pride across a host country seen in recent memory. In almost every way, Vancouver's Games were the opposite to Beijing's, certainly in the budgets involved— but if Beijing's goal was national reputation and identity-building, Vancouver's Games accomplished that in spades, without a single piece of iconic star-chitecture. . . .

What's best for Londoners to remember is that even for a great global city like theirs, the Olympics can be an incredible city and nation-changing moment—if it's designed that way, and the people embrace it. In the end, London will hopefully be remembered as a wonderful and joyous host city, and for what Canadian commentator Stephen Brunt called the quality and power of the "collective experience." There is power, and a lasting legacy, in that.

# 2

# Why No One Wants to Host the 2022 Olympics

*Dan Wetzel*

*Dan Wetzel is a writer at Yahoo! Sports.*

*Countries like Norway keep dropping out of the bidding for the 2022 Olympics. This is because potential host countries realize that staging the Olympics is enormously expensive, and that the International Olympic Committee (IOC), which controls the bidding process, is corrupt. The IOC demands unreasonable perks for its members and is suspected of accepting bribery. As long as the IOC continues to be corrupt and unaccountable, most countries are not going to want to host the Olympics.*

The surest sign that the bid process for hosting the Olympics is broken is actually not the trail of bribe money or crony-rich government contracts at the feet of International Olympic Committee members.

Sure, bribery might—might, maybe, allegedly, perhaps—be how a now abandoned Olympic Village got built in some muddy, bulldozed acreage south of Sochi, Russia, rather than in Salzburg, Austria, home to Mozart, the Sound of Music and postcard pictures.

That's the cause, though, not the effect.

The effect is the bidding for the 2022 Winter Games, which is now down to just two cities. The final vote comes next summer.

There's Beijing, China, which doesn't actually sit within 120 miles of a usable ski mountain, and there's Almaty, Kazakhstan, which in its bid touted itself as "the world's largest landlocked nation."

---

*Russia said it spent $51 billion hosting the 2014 Winter Olympics. What, no one else is interested in footing that bill?*

---

It's down to these two cities not because the IOC narrowed the field, but because every other city in the entire world said no.

Seriously, every other city said no.

That even includes cities that previously said yes and made it deep into the bidding process only to stare directly into the corrupt, humiliating voting system, not to mention eventual unnecessary construction costs, environmental effects, blown resources and white elephants built to opulent IOC code. They promptly high-tailed it the other way. Russia said it spent $51 billion hosting the 2014 Winter Olympics. What, no one else is interested in footing that bill?

Certainly not Oslo, Norway, not even at the bargain rate of an estimated $5.4 billion in a nation of just five million people. It once wanted desperately to host the 2022 Winter Olympics and its bid was so perfect that it was considered the favorite to win. Then the country held a vote earlier this year and 55.9 percent of Norwegians opposed.

Wednesday the Norwegian government effectively pulled the bid. Norwegians are known for the ability to cross country ski really fast and being so friendly they beg visitors to come experience their picturesque nation. Since this involved the IOC however, they decided against having visitors come experience their picturesque nation to watch them cross country ski really fast.

They aren't alone. Previous finalist Krakow, Poland, saw 70 percent voter opposition and pulled its application. A majority felt the same way in Germany and Switzerland, killing bids in Munich and St. Moritz respectively. In Sweden the majority party rejected funding the proposed games in Stockholm.

And that doesn't count all the places that didn't even bother to try, including the United States, which isn't sure when it will bid again after Chicago somehow, someway came in fourth in an effort to host the 2016 Summer Games. Rio de Janeiro won and still has practically nothing built, and IOC executives keep complaining nothing will be ready on time. Gee, what a shocker.

Essentially the only places interested in hosting the 2022 games are countries where actual citizens aren't allowed a real say in things—communist China and Kazakhstan, a presidential republic that coincidentally has only had one president since it split from the old USSR in 1989.

Essentially the entire world has told the IOC it's a corrupt joke.

"The vote is not a signal against the sport, but against the non-transparency and the greed for profit of the IOC," Ludwig Hartmann, a German politician said when his country said no. "I think all possible Olympic bids in Germany are now out of question. The IOC has to change first. It's not the venues that have to adapt to the IOC, but the other way around."

Don't hold your breath on that.

---

*If you think this is a crisis for the IOC, you don't know the IOC.*

---

It's worth noting there is nothing wrong with finding new places to host the games. The world changes. New nations gain power and money. Not everything has to be in Western Europe. Rising countries will do anything for the exposure.

China, for instance, is promising the construction of a super high-speed train to those far off mountains, even though Beijing is littered with abandoned venues from its 2008 Summer Games. Price doesn't matter.

And Almaty actually has a decent, viable and potentially winning bid. It looks like a good place for the Games, at least once you get past the Borat jokes—"Other Central Asian countries have inferior potassium."

Still, these are now the *only* choices.

If you think this is a crisis for the IOC, you don't know the IOC.

Oh, sure, president Thomas Bach said reform is needed for the bid process but this is a guy who spent his time in Sochi clinking champagne glasses with Vladimir Putin in an effort to help soften Vlad's global image. It worked for a week or so and Putin sent troops into the Ukraine. (How's that working out for you, Thomas?)

The IOC has billions of dollars laying around and billions more coming because to most people the Olympics is just a television show and the ratings are so high that the broadcast rights will never go down. The IOC doesn't pay the athletes. It doesn't share revenue with host countries. It doesn't pay for countries to send their athletes. It doesn't lay out any construction or capital costs. It doesn't pay taxes.

It basically holds caviar rich meetings in five star hotels in the Alps before calling it a day. That and conduct weak investigations into corruption charges of the bidding process, of course. "No evidence uncovered" is on a win streak.

It's a heck of a racket. Only FIFA does it better.

The world has caught on, though, which is why the mere mention of the IOC is toxic to all but the most desperate and totalitarian of governments.

The USOC is a non-governmental body, so unlike just about every other nation, it receives no direct public financing. It would love to host another Olympics, but the bid process is so unpredictable that wasting money and political capital on trying is risky. And then there would certainly be a public cost in the construction and hosting.

You want a good host for the 2022 Winter Olympics? Salt Lake City, which held it in 2002 and has all the venues and infrastructure already in place. There'd be some updating at minimal cost and, bang, a great location.

The IOC is too snooty for that, however. They don't like returning to the same city so soon so they'd prefer either Aspen, Colo. (complete with bullet train from Denver which has no practical use post Olympics) or Reno/Lake Tahoe. That would require billions building all the same stuff Salt Lake City already has in place.

Anyone want to put that up for a vote?

Then there is all the kissing up and glad-handing and who knows what else? Forget just the alleged direct payouts. How petty and ridiculous are these sporting aristocrats? Their actual listed demands are ridiculous, including their own airport entrance, traffic lane and prioritized stoplights. And just providing a five-star hotel suite isn't enough.

"IOC members will be received with a smile on arrival at hotel," the IOC demands. Instead the world is giving them the middle finger.

So China or Kazakhstan it is, the last two suckers on earth willing to step up to this carnival barker.

One lucky nation will win. The other will host the 2022 Winter Olympics.

# 3

# We're Still Lagging Behind in the Fight Against the Doping Cheats

*Rob Draper*

*Rob Draper is a writer for the* Daily Mail.

*Despite efforts to police drug use in sports, athletes who use illegal substances continue to slip past testing. More vigorous testing regimes are needed, and athletes need to be banned for longer periods if they test positive. As it is, athletes who tested positive in the past won many medals at the London 2012 Olympic Games. Many countries are not sufficiently committed to banning illegal substances; they want their athletes to compete and win medals, even when they are caught in violations.*

Drug cheats still prospered at London 2012 despite an unprecedented testing programme because Olympic sports still 'lag way behind' in the fight against doping, according to one of the most-respected anti-doping experts, Dick Pound.

His comments came as Belarus shot putter Nadezhda Ostapchuk was stripped of her gold medal for using steroids—the first medallist exposed as a cheat during the London Games—and US middle-distance runner Shannon Rowbury backed Britain's 1500m finalist Lisa Dobriskey in her claim that drug cheats had tainted the Games.

'We're lagging way behind,' said Pound, who was chairman of the World Anti-Doping Agency from its formation in 1999 to 2007.

'We know that with all the tests we're doing, 1.5–1.6 per cent of them are positive. There are far more people out there using drugs than we're catching, so why is that? We know there is more doping going on, so how come we're not getting it?'

Pound argues that the IOC should take seriously some of the claims by Victor Conte, who helped provide Dwain Chambers with his performance-enhancing drugs and was imprisoned for his part in the BALCO scandal for distributing performance-enhancing drugs, but who now says he wants to help root out cheats.

---

*Athletes now use small doses of testosterone, so-called micro dosing, so that they fall within the accepted ratio of testosterone allowed by testing.*

---

Pound insists that Conte's insight into the murky world of the drug cheats is valuable. 'I thought as someone trying to catch the cheats that it would be very helpful to know someone who knows what is going on, so I was very much in favour of building up a contact [with Conte]. My successor at WADA (Australian John Fahey) is a long way away and had no interest in Victor Conte, nor does David Howman (WADA chief executive).

'From time to time he [Conte] has come to me and said, "You're not doing the testing right".

'He said you have to get in there and test them in a certain window, in autumn and winter. Once they get on the circuit in the summer, you're not going to test them positive.'

Conte also says that athletes now use small doses of testosterone, so-called micro dosing, so that they fall within the accepted ratio of testosterone allowed by testing. Testosterone occurs naturally in the body but if an athlete has four times the accepted normal amount, it is deemed to be a doping offence.

Pound also hit out at sports federations that issue two-year bans for serious doping offences, when they already have the option to impose a four-year ban, claiming that the federations do so to protect doped athletes.

He said: 'We now have better evidence that a good steroid programme will last you two to four years, so we have a four-year ban. But most of the sports federations are not interested in it; they want the lower penalty because it doesn't keep their stars out of action so long. They don't care sports-performance wise.'

Dobriskey and Rowbury's complaints came after the women's 1500m Olympic final, which was won by Turkey's Asli Cakir Alptekin, who served a two-year ban for using EPO in 2004, and which saw Russia's Tatyana Tomashova, an athlete who served a two-year ban in 2008 for 'fraudulent substitution of urine' after a major undercover operation by the IAAF, athletics' governing body, finishing fourth.

A host of former drug cheats, including Britain's Dwain Chambers and David Millar, competed at the Games and gold medals were won by Kazakhstan cyclist Alexandre Vinokourov, Kazakhstan weightlifter Svetlana Podobedova, Belarussian swimmer Aliaksandra Herasimenia, Russian hammer thrower Tatyana Lysenko and Alptekin, who have all had positive drug tests.

Pound said: 'We all have to say that's not right and it should be a four-year ban.' Pound plays down the claims by Conte, made during the Olympics, that several athletes were using a new, undetectable substance. 'There was something he found which was being used in Europe,' said Pound.

'He managed to get some and we took to our lab in Montreal, which is one of the best. They looked at it but couldn't find anything in that substance that would be particularly useful to an athlete.'

The IOC conducted more than 6,000 blood and urine tests during the Olympics, catching out nine athletes.

But 117 were caught out by anti-doping agencies in the run-up to the Games since April. WADA insist that they are taking the issue of micro-dosing seriously. A WADA spokesman said: 'The issue of micro-dosing is nothing new to WADA. It presents a challenge to the anti-doping movement as cheaters have become more sophisticated.

'Micro-dosing can involve a range of different substances and not just synthetic testosterone. We have alerted all to these matters so that science can deal with the challenge.'

WADA point out that its rules have already reduced the ratio of permitted testosterone from 6:1 to 4:1, but admit that anti-doping agencies do have the right to test any sample, even if it falls below the 4:1 ratio.

# 4

# Performance-Enhancing Drugs Should Be Allowed in the Olympics

*Ian Steadman*

*Ian Steadman is a writer for* Wired *magazine.*

*Doping is impossible to consistently detect, and all major cycling champions have been implicated in doping. Given this, it seems like it would make sense to simply legalize doping and other performance-enhancing drugs. This would make drug use safer, since athletes could use substances openly and could receive better medical care. Nor would it violate the spirit of sport, since athletes already use various methods (clothing, training) to improve performance. As drugs in everyday life become more common, sports will move toward a greater acceptance of performance-enhancing drugs.*

Poor old Lance Armstrong. The seven-time Tour de France winner is likely to have all those famous victories taken away from him, after accusations by the United States Anti-Doping Agency that he used illicit performance enhancing drugs. He never tested positive for anything, but his decision not to fight his corner has been taken as tantamount to a confession. And why shouldn't he be punished? Doping is, after all, the ultimate sin of the professional athlete.

## Switch to Pro-Doping

Dwain Chambers, the UK's fastest sprinter in the 100m race, was banned from competing in the Olympic Games after testing positive for the anabolic steroid tetrahydrogestrinone—and even if his ban was overturned, he claimed in his autobiography that at least half of the US racing team at Beijing 2008 were using illegal substances. The battle to control drug use never, ever seems to end. So, why don't we accept doping will always happen, and legalise it? It may seem a crazy idea, but a switch to a pro-doping culture might be the inevitable future of sport.

---

*We should embrace the inevitable, and control doping as best we can.*

---

It gets to the heart of what it is we want when we compete and watch sport, and also what we consider to be "normal" humanity. An athlete who takes a performance enhancing drug is relying on something that they don't themselves have to improve their performance—whether that drug is naturally occurring or designed by scientists, whether that extra help skews their genetics to alter their humanity.

As training, coaching, nutrition and equipment has been perfected, the best times of the best athletes have been increasing at a slower and slower rate. There are numerous estimates of what the fastest possible 100m time will be, based on extrapolating current trends—the most recent study found that 9.48 was the predicted "fastest" time.

Eventually, natural athletes will reach a wall, and there comes the question of how to keep sport interesting. We could start measuring to the thousandth of a second, say, but how interesting would it be for spectators if every race came down to a difference undetectable to the naked eye? There's no narrative of success there, nothing as iconic as Usain Bolt strolling across the line in Beijing with the swagger of a man who knows he has utterly destroyed his competition. Such accuracy is also difficult to pull off in places like swimming pools, for instance, where distances of a couple of millimetres may be needed to decide a race. The concrete in current pools wasn't built for that kind of margin of error.

That's where doping comes in. After all, it's not like it's going to go away, argues practical ethics professor Julian Savulescu: "The war on doping has failed. Lance Armstrong never failed a doping test, despite being subjected to thousands. Nearly every recent winner of the Tour de France has been implicated in doping. About 80 percent of 100m finalists are or will be implicated in doping. The fact is that blood doping and use of growth hormone have not been possible to detect, and because doping mimics normal physiological process it will always be possible to beat the test." Thus, we should embrace the inevitable, and control doping as best we can.

This is a view echoed by bioethicist professor Andy Miah, who argues that we should have a "World Pro-Doping Agency" to complement the World Anti-Doping Agency (WADA): "At the moment athletes look to find dangerous substances with significant health risks, but with the correct framework in place athletes can know the risks involved."

---

*Performance enhancing drugs are [the] great leveller, that tool for athletes to bridge the unfair natural gap.*

---

## Pro-Doping Is Safer

It makes sense to make sure that athletes know what they are ingesting, as opposed to the current free-for-all which can lead to awful side effects for athletes. Anabolic steroids, for instance, have adverse side effects which range from acne, infertility and impotence, to hypertension, psychosis and cardiovascular disease. A regulatory body that lets athletes know what they're ingesting would improve athletic health.

However, this doesn't address the issue of authenticity and integrity that professional sport is built upon. After all, Bradley Wiggins could easily get up a mountain faster if he was using a motorbike. Our societal conception of sport as competition between opponents rests on a certain sense of human nature—what will decide the battle is determination, and effort, and grit, and sweat. We can help the honest athlete compete with the doper by allowing both to use drugs, but that seems to start picking apart why we value sport.

Savulescu doesn't see this as a problem: "Steroids augment the effects of training. They are like more effective training, which has been achieved in other ways. That does not corrupt the nature of sport. Caffeine is a performance enhancer which was banned but is now allowed. The relaxation has done nothing to affect the spectacle, nature or definition of sport. It has just meant we don't have to waste time working out how much Coca-Cola an athlete has drunk."

People still need to train to make the most of their drugs, then. It doesn't help to look at sport as being a battle of wills if, as we've already seen, the natural limits of the human body are increasingly the reason for success. I could try all I want, but I will never make it as a professional gymnast because I'm just too tall and awkward. The same applies to many athletes now who are never going to be able to beat [British track and field star] Jessica Ennis, no matter how much they try.

We—as spectators—push athletes to be the absolute best, and in the process create the culture where doping is needed to reach those heights. It increasingly feels difficult to reconcile the purity of asking athletes to do whatever it takes to win as long as that isn't going beyond an arbitrary definition of "natural." Performance enhancing drugs are that great leveller, that tool for athletes to bridge the unfair natural gap.

## In the Spirit of Sport

Savulescu agrees: "Doping is not against the spirit of sport. It has always been part of the human spirit to use knowledge to make oneself better and doping has been a part of sport since its beginning. Doping should only be banned when it is significantly harmful relative to the inherent risks of sport, or against the spirit of a particular sport. For example, drugs to reduce tremor like betablockers in archery or shooting are against the spirit of that sport as it is inherently a test of ability to control nerves. Drugs which removed fear in boxing would be against the spirit of boxing. But blood doping up to a haematocrit [percentage of red blood cells in blood] of 50 percent is safe and not against the spirit of cycling."

Miah also points out that there is a lot of legal doping going on already—such as altitude chambers, which recreate the experience of training in thinner air to give athletes a bigger oxygen capacity. The WADA approved such chambers in 2006 because they were felt to recreate a natural phenomenon—but then what's the difference between that and injecting someone with natural growth hormones, for instance?

This points towards the fundamental problem many have with doping—its implications for what it is to be human. Athletics is at the forefront of that debate. Just look at Oscar Pistorius.

*We can see—from the use of drugs by students to improve studying to the medication of children to keep them calm—that personal enhancement through drugs is more and more common.*

"He symbolises the coming together of the two Olympic movements," says Miah. "If [International Olympic Committee founder] Pierre de Cobourtin founded the Olympic movement today, seeing how the gap between [the Olympic and Paralympic Games] is closing, there would be only one Games."

Pistorius represents a future where our ability to transcend what a "normal" human being is will also herald the end of a distinction between the abled and the disabled—and drugs are a big part of that.

That's because, as Miah points out, human enhancement will become more and more common in everyday life. "The current problems will become less apparent because the athletes of the future will be enhanced before they even begin training for an event," he says. "Look at the human genome, for instance—twenty years ago it took thousands of dollars to sequence just one man, now it costs $5,000 (£3,135). That process will only get cheaper. The continual pursuit of enhanced life will lead to these things becoming normalised."

## Personal Enhancement Through Drugs

We can see—from the use of drugs by students to improve studying to the medication of children to keep them calm—that personal enhancement through drugs is more and more common. As genetic profiling becomes more common, too, that will also herald huge changes as people are screened for diseases at birth that they may only have come to discover in later life. You can already see this as an issue when it comes to so-called "gene doping," where techniques used in gene therapy may be used to switch on or off certain genes associated with, for instance, improved muscle mass, or faster acceleration.

Doping, then, becomes part of the grand question that humanity is beginning to ask itself as nature is increasingly improved upon with technology. Just as innovations in Formula 1 cars eventually filter down to your humble hatchback, those pills and serums that athletes take to shave another 0.01 second off a personal best may well herald a common life enhancing drug later down the line.

"What is a normal human?" asks Miah. "Athletes in the NFL have 20/15 vision, which is better than normal. People are concerned about genetic identification, that the use of ge-

netic tests will be normal. People may recoil from that, think-
ing that it may compromise what it means to be human, but I
don't think it changes any kind of internal human essence."

That may be the crux. If there were to be an Olympiad in,
let's say . . . thirty years' time, then will there be a Paralympiad
alongside? Or will there in fact be three, with a new Olympiad
for those who choose to enhance their bodies beyond what
they were born with? Whatever happens, it will be a reflection
of wider society's attitudes towards human enhancement beyond what is natural, or normal.

# The Sochi Olympics Are an Environmental Disaster

*McKenzie Funk*

*McKenzie Funk is the author of* Windfall: The Booming Business of Global Warming.

*Russian president Vladimir Putin often engages in environmentally destructive building projects for his personal luxury or enjoyment. Environmental activists oppose him, but they are often targeted for oppression or bullying by the state. For example, the Olympic building for Sochi is destroying wetlands and damaging people's homes. Protest has been ineffective, as Putin simply ignores protestors or threatens and intimidates them.*

Members of the RGS [a Russian scientific club] worked with local environmental groups to publicly voice concerns about the [Sochi] Olympics, but the hall they reserved was suddenly made unavailable, supposedly because of an accidental double booking. Another press conference, planned for the seashore adjacent to the new stadiums and disappearing wetland, was blocked by the government construction firm Olympstroy, which soon won a permanent injunction that effectively made certain public beaches private. To get the word out, members published articles in journals and on the club's website, and they did as many media interviews as they could.

## Moscow Targets Protestors

All of which attracted Moscow's attention. In late 2009, the national leadership of the RGS called an extraordinary meeting: it had been decided that the organization needed a new charter. Under the proposal, branch offices would be stripped of their independent legal status. They would now get funding—and marching orders—from regional offices, which in turn would take orders from a new office of the executive director, based in Moscow. In effect, the RGS would be federalized—and the Sochi branch muzzled. In a separate vote, Sergei Shoigu, Russia's minister of emergencies and a prominent member of [Vladimir] Putin's United Russia party, was elected the new president of the RGS. Until that day, he had not even been a member. Putin himself was given the surprise invitation to chair its board of trustees, which he accepted in a speech before the delegates.

---

*Stalin wouldn't have let this event happen . . . because it's just ruining the city.*

---

"We are now the last branch that is not part of the new system," [geologist] Maria [Reneva] said. Any day now, a lawsuit would come from Moscow—they had been told it was imminent—and local officials were already making vague threats. "If we don't join, we will have 'problems,'" Maria said. Problems with their papers, problems with their taxes—whatever problems authorities wanted to find. Under the new charter, RGS branches could not own property, and the Sochi branch's seaside house could be worth millions to the right oligarch. Just up the hill, glass-walled palaces were under construction along the road to Stalin's dacha; they were rumored to belong to the local governor, another United Russia stalwart, who would use them to host guests during the Olympics. Maria and [ecologist] Yulia [Naberezhnova] were trying to carry on as usual as they awaited the lawsuit. They told [photographer] Simon [Roberts] and me that the branch's monthly show-and-tell, which featured slide shows and expedition reports from regular members, would take place the coming Sunday. And if we wanted a reality tour of Olympic venues, they could give us one the day after tomorrow. . . .

## Stalin and Sochi

[Former Russian dictator Josef] Stalin seemed to love Sochi as much as Putin does. "What would Stalin think about the Olympics coming to Sochi?" Simon asked.

"Stalin wouldn't have let this event happen," she said, "because it's just ruining the city." [Russian leader Vladimir Putin] also has a Sochi dacha—three, in fact, if rumors are to be believed. The rumors are backed up by property records, leaks from whistle-blowers, federal guards at the fence lines, and photos taken by activists and construction workers and posted online. Everyone in Sochi accepted them as settled truth. At least five people—scientists, translators, mountaineers—told me they had seen a secret presidential residence with their own eyes.

One of the dachas, a $350 million Italianate mansion known as Putin's Palace, was on the Black Sea coast north of Sochi. Another was in the woods behind Krasnaya Polyana, close to the site for the 2014 downhill-skiing events. But the one I wanted to visit was more than 6,000 feet up the snowy flanks of the highest peak in the western Caucasus, 9,363-foot Mount Fisht, the namesake of the main Olympic stadium. The place was called Lunnaya Polyana, or Moonglade, and depending on whose map you believed, it was either inside or on the border of a protected Unesco World Heritage site— "one of the few large mountain areas of Europe that has not experienced significant human impacts," Unesco pointed out when the western Caucasus were chosen for designation in 1999.

Once construction of a main lodge began in 2002, the site was officially listed as a weather station or a "scientific center" and given the name Biosphere. But then came ski lifts and helipads and Swiss-style architecture and multiple chalets and dozens of guest rooms and four new snowcats, and it became clear that Moonglade was something else: an elite private ski resort inside a onetime wilderness. There were no passable roads here; construction materials were brought by helicopter, presumably at enormous cost. Someone had nevertheless found room in the budget for flatscreen televisions, a moose head, a swimming pool, and at least two billiard tables.

---

*Moonglade was one of 20 palaces and country cottages that Putin had available for his personal use, along with four yachts, 15 helicopters, and 43 aircraft.*

---

After pictures of Moonglade appeared online, Putin's press secretary said his experiences there were "exactly" like those of "ordinary tourists." It was an odd statement, since ordinary tourists lack helicopters, and if they came to Mount Fisht at all it was during summer, when they could follow once popular Soviet trekking routes through fields of flowers and into the stunning high country.

Hikers had been some of the first to notice the strange construction at Moonglade. Some reported being chased off by guards who forced them to delete photos from their cameras. Images got out anyway, thanks in large part to the homegrown group Environment Watch on the North Caucasus, or EWNC, which began hiking to Moonglade for annual "inspections" in 2007. Photos and surreptitiously shot video appeared. In Moscow, opposition leaders added Moonglade to a list of increasingly lavish presidential perks that they cataloged in a 2012 report called "The Life of a Galley Slave." The title was a reference to something Putin declared after his first turn as president: "All these eight years I toiled like a galley slave,

from morning until evening, with every ounce of my strength."
According to the report, Moonglade was one of 20 palaces
and country cottages that Putin had available for his personal
use, along with four yachts, 15 helicopters, and 43 aircraft.
The authors enlarged photos of Putin's wrist taken during
various public appearances and identified a watch collection
worth roughly $657,000—more than six times his official an-
nual salary.

I had arrived in Sochi with ski-touring gear, a map of
Mount Fisht, and a half-baked plan to do a Moonglade inspection of my own—but the same rains that ruined various
Olympic test events scuttled my chances. Jeep roads to the
trailhead were impassably muddy, there wasn't enough snow
to move quickly on skis, and the mountain guides I called
laughed at my plan, saying it would take me most of a week
to hike up Mount Fisht and back. So I settled for an evening
train trip northwest along the Black Sea to meet the founder
of EWNC, Audrey Rudomakha, a legendary Caucasus activist
who was perhaps the region's most persistent thorn in Putin's
side. My train mates passed the time smoking, drinking tea,
and talking loudly on their cell phones. But when sunset came
and we passed empty pebble beaches lapped by dark waves,
everyone stared out the windows and there was a moment of
reverent silence.

## An Environmental Disaster

At the station in Krasnodar, the regional capital, a group of
college-age men met me with a cardboard sign that read
STATE DEPARTMENT. One explained the joke: "Everyone
thinks we're funded by America." Dissent in Russia was increasingly maligned as a foreign plot, and Putin had just
signed a controversial law saying that any organization that
receives money from abroad has to state clearly on paper and
electronic documents that it is a "foreign agent." My hosts and
I piled into a junker Lada with a missing seat and raced to the

small offices of Yabloko, or Apple, a green political party. Politics were Rudomakha's latest experiment, an attempt—not yet very successful—to see if there was a way to fight for the Caucasus beyond picket lines and press releases.

Inside, young volunteers were devouring pizza while Rudomakha—in his youth a rock guitarist, Che Guevara admirer, and founder of a commune—typed quietly at a computer. His goatee and trademark pile of dark hair were now trimmed, almost respectable. He and I grabbed slices and sat down in the kitchen. The Olympics, Rudomakha told me, were an environmental disaster that he and the EWNC were protesting at every turn. Moonglade was just as "ecologically dangerous," because the area had formerly been so pristine, but it was also where Rudomakha had achieved a major victory. A few years ago, authorities started to build a paved road to Moonglade through the heart of the wilderness, and the EWNC filed a lawsuit, sent activists to block machinery and loggers, and made an emergency appeal to Unesco. A public warning by Unesco that it might have to add the western Caucasus to its list of threatened World Heritage sites was enough to get the road canceled, even if the ski lodge remained, and even if a fight now loomed over a different road project, to access Moonglade from the other side. "There is no law in Russia," Rudomakha said. "That's why most of our fights are fights to lose. But this has Unesco. We may have a chance."

Why did the oligarchs need a road at all, I wondered, when they had helicopters? "National security," Rudomakha explained. According to yet another rumor, impossible to confirm, Putin once became stuck at the dacha when a winter storm grounded his chopper. He had to go back down the mountain on foot, like an ordinary tourist. That was unacceptable.

Rudomakha had hiked in to inspect Moonglade four times, and with each visit he saw more security. Most recently, he said, there was a fence and a watchtower. Rudomakha's deputy, a clean-shaven man named Dima, pulled out a laptop to show me on Google Maps how to find Putin's palace on the Black Sea, which also occupied public land and was surrounded by a tall fence. Dima told the story of a time when he and another well-known EWNC activist, the biologist Suren Gazaryan, made an inspection of the palace. Inside, they came across a surprised security guard and a man in camouflage, who told Dima he was an officer in the presidential guard.

"What is the Presidential Security Service doing here?" Dima asked.

---

*Soon the news would trickle out that Russia had set up a surveillance system in Sochi that would monitor every tweet, e-mail, and phone call made by visitors during the Olympics.*

---

"None of your business," the man replied.

Officers from the FSB, the successor to the [Soviet security service] KGB, appeared, along with border guards, although any border is over a hundred miles away. Then came local police and men from a private security company. "They took all our cameras," Dima said, "and suddenly there was no mobile-phone service. They broke into Suren's car and took notebooks, laptops, phones, modems—everything electrical."

The activists were taken to a police station to give a written explanation of what they were doing in the supposedly public forest. "I saved one memory card in a sock," Dima said. "It was the only media that survived." Gazaryan was later convicted for damage to a construction fence—someone had painted THIS IS OUR FOREST! on it—then charged with attempted murder because he had picked up a small rock and told a security guard to keep his distance. Facing years in prison, he fled Russia in November 2012 and is now in exile in Estonia.

## Olympic Sites

"Do you have just one daughter, Yulia?" I asked her this on a rainy morning as we set out with Maria to do the RGS tour of Olympic sites. It was just small talk, but she wheeled around in the front seat of the car and stared fiercely at me. "How did you know that?" she demanded. She calmed down when I reminded her that I had seen the little girl at the RGS branch earlier in the week, but in an instant I understood the atmosphere of fear that now pervaded everything. Soon the news would trickle out that Russia had set up a surveillance system in Sochi that would monitor every tweet, e-mail, and phone call made by visitors during the Olympics.

Yulia, I learned, was also a longtime member of the EWNC; she had even lived on Rudomakha's commune in the nineties. Rudomakha and Gazaryan, meanwhile, were RGS members as well as EWNC leaders. But it was important that I distinguish between the two groups, Maria said. The Sochi RGS's opposition to the Games wasn't in any way political; it had everything to do with what we were about to see.

Our destination was an important wetland for migrating birds—some 200 documented species, Yulia said, plus various rare plants. A decade ago, she and the RGS spent a year and a half leading a detailed survey of flora and fauna. She handed me an old brochure showing frogs, ferns, swans, and the snowy Caucasus reflected in the deep blue of a pristine pond. "This territory was going to be a preserve," she said. "We had all the documents prepared. It was going to be protected by the Ramsar wetlands treaty. Then it was gone."

We turned off the highway and followed a line of giant orange dump trucks into the Coastal Cluster. Fisht and other partly built Olympic stadiums were rising out of the mud, surrounded by gravel roads and a growing forest of high-rise housing for athletes, media, and spectators. The din of construction was audible even through the closed windows of the car. Maria groaned. Yulia peered out the window. "It's hard to say in one word how this makes me feel," she said. "I want to be a giant and take all the buildings and trucks and break them." She made a snapping motion with her hands. "It is horrible to make such things with nature."

"We say this area is like Oman," Maria said. "It has become like a desert, with no trees."

---

*Up to 30,000 tons of Olympic debris, most of it from railroad construction, ended up in an illegal landfill.*

---

When we got to what remained of the wetland, Maria and Yulia said nothing. They didn't need to. A series of barren ponds marked the intersection of two mud tracks plied by a steady rush of trucks. Their banks were littered with plastic bottles, construction debris, and piles of slash wood. A stray dog stood next to two portable toilets, and next to the toilets were two signs, one in Russian, one in English, that declared this apocalyptic scene the NATURAL ORNITHOLOGICAL PARK IMERETINSKAYA LOWLAND.

"On the whole territory of the Natural Park," said the signs, "it is prohibited to perform actions leading to changing its historically formed natural landscape." Habitat for animal species—above all, endangered species—had to be preserved. Specifically, one could not hunt, damage breeding spots, harvest wild plants, pollute the water with raw sewage, or decrease the "ecological, aesthetical, and recreational qualities of the Natural Park." The cynicism was almost brave.

From the wetland, we drove to a residential neighborhood overlooking the Coastal Cluster, stopping only for water and bread at a gas station. Yulia ate her portion in the rain in the parking lot. We were looking for a street called Bakinskaya that neither Maria nor Yulia had ever visited, but it wasn't hard to recognize once we found it. An entire block of homes, most of them still occupied, were tilted at strange angles, as if Yulia's angry giant had swung and missed the Olympic site and hit these houses instead. Just downhill, two apartment buildings looked like Sochi's version of Pisa: they leaned drunkenly toward one another, propping each other up.

## Olympic Debris

For two years, residents here had watched dump trucks arrive full at the top of the hill above them, then return empty. Up to 30,000 tons of Olympic debris, most of it from railroad construction, ended up in an illegal landfill. One day, after a rain, the hillside suddenly slipped, and all the homes' foundations slipped along with it. Ten months before we visited, the government had finally agreed to resettle Bakinskaya's residents. But ten months had passed, and the dump trucks kept dumping, and the people were still living in their slumping homes. A man Simon and I met on the street told us that he feared more landslides. Why not move? "I spent all my money on this house," he said. He couldn't afford to go anywhere else.

Our last stop—new to Maria but not to Yulia—was an activist encampment on the north bank of the Kudepsta River, manned 24 hours a day by local residents and the occasional EWNC member. They had occupied the site for nine months, ever since a construction company put a temporary bridge here and prepared to drive heavy equipment over it. A 367-megawatt gas-fired electrical plant was to be built on the other side to power the 2014 Games. The activists, many of them pensioners in fraying sweaters who sat around a stove in a shelter made of tarps and scrap wood, feared that its noise and air pollution would alter the neighborhood forever.

They were holding a press conference today. A few minutes after we arrived, two leaders—one wearing a Yabloko jacket—began speaking to a crowd of perhaps 50 people who had gathered at the bridge. For 20 minutes they seemed formidable, ready to throw their bodies in front of the machinery again if it came rolling across the bridge. But after the local journalists left, the gathering became a discussion about strategy, and then the discussion became a bitter argument about tactics. As the rain poured down, the argument nearly came to blows. Maria led Simon and me to the car. "How can they ever win?" Simon mused. Democracy was laudable. Compared with Putinism, it was also frail.

# Israel Should Have Boycotted Sochi over Russia's Anti-Gay Record

*Goel Pinto*

*Goel Pinto is a journalist who writes for the Israeli newspaper Haaretz.*

*The anti-gay legislation in Russia is comparable in some ways to the anti-Jewish legislation passed in Hitler's Germany. Israel should take a stand against bigotry and discrimination and boycott the Sochi Olympic Games. If that is not possible, individual Israelis should at least boycott Olympic sponsors. It is important for Israel and Israelis to make it clear that discrimination and hatred against minority groups are not acceptable.*

Everyone knows about Jesse Owens, the African-American track star who won four gold medals at the 1936 Berlin Summer Olympics, striking a blow against Nazi theories of Aryan racial superiority in the process. Less well-known is the story of two other track and field competitors, Marty Glickman and Sam Stoller, who were sidelined by the U.S. Olympic committee in an effort to appease Adolf Hitler.

## Hitler and Putin

It would be inconceivable today for participating countries to bar athletes from next February's [2014] Winter Olympics in Sochi to avoid incurring the wrath of the Russians. And

Moscow's anti-gay laws are not the Nuremberg Laws [the Nazi anti-Jewish laws]. It is nevertheless fitting for the world to draw a parallel between the two Olympic settings, past and future.

Earlier this year Russia passed homophobic laws that boil down to this: You can be gay-lesbian-transgender, just don't "propagandize homosexualism." And if you leave your home holding your gay partner's hand or wearing a pin that identifies you as gay, you can be thrown in jail. These laws gave dangerous Russian groups, most of them neo-Nazi, [permission] to beat up and humiliate gays throughout the country.

As a result of these laws, critical questions have been raised regarding the Sochi Olympics. The major one is whether it is appropriate to use the doomsday weapon of a boycott, when its main victims would be the citizens and not the government of the target state. Another issue is whether a boycott would be effective, that is, result in the repeal of the homophobic laws or in a change in public awareness. In the case of Russia, according to a recent poll 88 percent of Russians support the legislation.

---

*It's not clear what would happen if two competitors of the same sex go for a stroll along the Black Sea beach hand-in-hand next February and are spotted by the [Russian] police.*

---

The fact of the Olympics' taking place in a fascist state that passes homophobic laws obliges the leaders of other countries and of the International Olympic Committee to address several issues.

World leaders, most notably U.S. President Barack Obama, have already announced that they will not boycott the games. (Although he added that he hoped gay athletes would win gold medals in Sochi). The heads of the IOC [International Olympic Committee] did what they always do: cover their greed and lust for power with declarations of principle, such as sports being above politics. They also trotted out Rule 50 of the Olympic charter, according to which: "No kind of demonstration or political, religious or racial propaganda is permitted in any Olympic sites, venues or other areas."

IOC officials also say the Russian authorities have assured them that the laws will not apply to visiting athletes. But the Russians actually issued a declaration stating that all tourists, including Olympic competitors, are obliged to observe the laws of the country they are visiting and that the legislation in question will apply to foreigners and Russian citizens alike.

It's not clear what would happen if two competitors of the same sex go for a stroll along the Black Sea beach hand-in-hand next February and are spotted by the police. Will the police beat them, as they beat gay demonstrators at protests this year? Will they jail them, as has been done since the homophobic laws took effect? Perhaps their Olympic attire would protect them.

These questions apply not only to the Olympics but also to other international events due to take place in Russia, such as the Miss Universe pageant in November [2013] and the 2018 soccer World Cup.

## Protest in Some Form

In any event it is appropriate that the Jewish state at least deliberate the issue and come out strongly and clearly against the discrimination and violations of human rights taking place in Russia. And if the State of Israel doesn't do anything, we as individuals can act. In a world in which there are no longer people with moral values, and those with money remain the only ones in control, one can at least conduct an individual, personal boycott of the international companies sponsoring the Olympics. Perhaps in that way, those firms will understand that while they boast how they are bringing nations together, we are bringing people together.

# Arguments for Boycotting Sochi Are Unconvincing

*Ilya Somin*

*Ilya Somin is a professor at the George Mason University School of Law and an adjunct scholar at the Cato Institute.*

*A boycott of the Russian Olympics in Sochi would deny the Russians a propaganda victory, and would be more effective in that regard than simply attending the games and registering disapproval. However, Russia's human rights record, though bad, is no worse than many other countries that have hosted the games, such as China. Perhaps the games should only be hosted by liberal democracies. But since that is not the current standard, it does not make sense to boycott Russia in particular.*

Gay rights advocates such as actor Harvey Fierstein are calling for a boycott of the 2014 Winter Olympics in Sochi, Russia, over Russia's highly repressive new law banning "homosexual propaganda," any speech that equates the social status of same-sex relationships with heterosexual ones. Others argue that the West should not boycott the Olympics, but should instead use it as an opportunity to highlight Russia's abuses of gay rights. Russian officials have given conflicting statements about whether the law will be enforced against gay athletes and foreign visitors during the games.

Ilya Somin, "Should We Boycott the Olympics?" *Volokh Conspiracy*, August 5, 2013. Copyright © 2013 The Volokh Conspiracy. All rights reserved. Reproduced with permission.

## Boycott Prevents Propaganda Victory

The anti-gay crackdown is just one of many human rights abuses undertaken by the regime of ex-KGB Colonel Vladimir Putin. Others include repression of opposition media and persecution of critics of the government. Indeed, the government's promotion of homophobia is just one facet of its broader ideology of authoritarian nationalism.

In terms of promoting the cause of human rights in Russia, I suspect that a boycott would be more effective than merely calling attention to abuses, while simultaneously attending the Games. Hosting the Olympics is nearly always a propaganda victory for the government of the nation where they take place. Even an otherwise corrupt and inefficient government can put on an impressive dog and pony show that draws favorable media coverage, if given years to prepare. The nation that gave the world the concept of the Potemkin Village is surely no exception.

---

*To conclude that Russia is an unfit host for the Olympics because of its human rights record is essentially to say that only liberal democracies should be allowed to host such events.*

---

A boycott has a greater chance of effectively punishing Russia for its unjust policies, and stimulating pressure for change. Sports boycotts against South Africa may have helped hasten the fall of apartheid. The boycott of the 1980 Moscow Olympics by the US and sixty other nations is often seen as a failure because it did not put an end to the Soviet invasion of Afghanistan. But it did deny a brutal totalitarian regime what would have been a valuable propaganda victory. Some argue that the US was right not to boycott the 1936 Olympics in Nazi Germany, because it led to victories by Jesse Owens and other black athletes, which contradicted Nazi ideology. At the time, however, the Berlin Olympics were generally perceived as a propaganda success for the Third Reich.

## Why Russia Is Not Unique

But in deciding whether a boycott is defensible, it's worth keeping in mind that, bad as it is, Russia's human rights record is no worse than that of numerous other authoritarian and quasi-authoritarian governments. Unlike its communist predecessor, today's Russian government allows some degree of freedom for opposition movements, and does not engage in mass murder. As recently as 2008, the summer Olympics were held in China, a nation ruled by a regime with an even worse human rights record than Russia's, including the forcible expulsion of over one million people from their homes in order to prepare for the Olympic Games themselves. Yet there were few calls for a boycott in 2008, and those few were largely ignored. Many other governments, particularly in the Muslim world, also have antigay policies harsher than Russia's.

To conclude that Russia is an unfit host for the Olympics because of its human rights record is essentially to say that only liberal democracies should be allowed to host such events. Maybe that should indeed be the standard. I tentatively lean in that direction myself. But we should be clear about the principles involved and try to apply them consistently.

Obviously, we could instead conclude that repression of gays and lesbians justifies a boycott, but violations of other human rights do not. I'm a strong supporter of gay and lesbian equality. But I don't see any justification for such a double standard. It is wrong for Russia to punish "gay propaganda." But it is no less wrong for it to engage in various other kinds of unjust censorship on a comparable or greater scale. It's not obvious to me that Russia's oppression of gays and lesbians falls in a qualitatively different category from, say, China's oppression of the Tibetans.

UPDATE: One possible argument against boycotting the Sochi Olympics—or any Olympics—is the traditional idea that international sports events should be free of politics, and therefore should not be used to make a political point. This is a potentially attractive principle. The problem is that the Olympics are virtually always used as a propaganda tool by the host government. For that reason, it is nearly impossible to make them genuinely politically neutral. Unfortunately, the only realistic options are either to allow repressive regimes to use the games to burnish their public image, keep them from hosting them in the first place, or undercut their propaganda by means of a boycott widespread enough to undercut the games' public relations benefits for the hosts.

UPDATE #2: It is perhaps worth noting that the Russian government's antigay policies are in line with majority public opinion in that country, which is very homophobic.

# 8

# The Olympics Have Always Been a Venue for Political Protest

*Tracy Smith*

*Tracy Smith is a correspondent for* CBS News Sunday Morning.

*Many people feel that the Olympics should not be a place for politics. However, there have always been political statements and political protests at the Olympics. In the 2014 Olympics at Sochi, President Barack Obama sent a delegation including gay athletes to protest Russia's anti-gay policies. In the 1980 Olympic Games, the US victory in hockey over Russia was seen as a triumph in the Cold War. In 1968, American sprinters John Carlos and Tommie Smith raised their gloved hands on the medal podium in a black power salute, a gesture that was controversial and has become iconic. In one way or another, therefore, politics will remain part of the Olympic Games.*

Aren't politicking and activism at the Olympics supposed to be out of bounds? Despite what the rules say, the reality is frequently quite different. Our Cover Story is reported now by Tracy Smith:

At 50, Brian Boitano hardly seems to have lost his edge. Twenty-six years after winning the figure skating gold medal at the 1988 Olympics, he has a new role at the 2014 Winter

Tracy Smith, "Politics at the Olympics: Out of Bounds?" CBS News, February 9, 2014. Copyright © 2015 CBS Interactive Inc. All rights reserved. Reproduced with permission.

Games, as one of three openly gay athletes named to a nine-person official delegation representing the U.S. at the Sochi Olympics.

## Boitano and Gay Rights

"I didn't realize that President [Barack] Obama was sending such an immense message through this delegation," he said.

"And you, at that moment, were not openly gay?" said Smith.

"No, I was not, at that moment, openly gay. And I had no plans to," Boitano said. "Not because I was ashamed or anything, but because I realize I have a public side of my life, but I also have a personal side of my life."

But he was told years ago that appearances count and successful athletes need to maintain a certain image.

---

*It seems that whenever the world's athletes gather, politics goes along for the ride—and in Sochi it's been especially rough.*

---

"After the Olympics, I had an agent who said, 'I don't know if you're gay or not, but you need to go on TV and say that you're not gay, because I'm trying to get you projects and endorsements,'" Boitano said.

Still, he decided that if ever there was a time to make a statement, this would be it.

So what, to him, is the message? "Everybody is different. And just because, you know, we're gay, does not mean that we can't be successful and we can't be proud, we can't be strong. We're all of those things—and we are Americans."

It seems that whenever the world's athletes gather, politics goes along for the ride—and in Sochi it's been especially rough.

First, the games are being held under threat of attack by Islamic militants, including the group that pulled off an attack in Volgograd last year; and relations between the U.S. and Russia are strained at best.

And then there's this: last year, the Russians passed a law banning what they call "gay propaganda": basically, they've made it illegal to express any gay rights sentiment in public.

That prompted President Obama to round out the U.S. delegation with gay athletes. Besides Boitano, there's tennis great Billie Jean King and hockey medalist Caitlin Cahow.

It comes down to a clash of cultures, according to NYU Russian Studies professor Stephen Cohen.

"You're dealing with a different civilization, to a certain extent," Cohen said, "cause it's half in Europe, half in Asia, a country where 19th century traditions are very, very strong, where the Orthodox Church is very, very strong, and change comes in these societies from within.

"The problem is, politics has intruded more so than any Olympics I can remember."

## Miracle on Ice

Truth is, politics has always been part of the Olympics. The U.S. boycotted the 1980 Summer Olympic Games in Moscow over the Soviet invasion of Afghanistan. And then there was the 1980 Winter Olympics in Lake Placid, N.Y., when a hockey game between the U.S. and the Soviet teams became a Cold War showdown.

Mike Eruzione was 25 then, and captain of the team the whole country was watching.

"There was a telegram from a lady in Texas," he told Smith, "and all the telegram said was, 'Beat those commie bastards.' And it had nothing to do with the hockey game. But that was the mindset of people who weren't hockey fans. And I think that's what kind of made the moment so special for so many people."

And "special" doesn't even begin to describe it:

The U.S. team defeated the Soviets with a score of 4-3. The victory, known then and forever as the "Miracle on Ice," triggered an outburst of national pride.

---

*I'd like to tell you it was this clearly political moment, but it was never talked about in the locker room.*

---

"So everybody had had a different meaning," said Eruzione. "For us as a hockey team, we won. But for a nation, we won."

But Eruzione says making a political statement was the last thing on his mind.

"For us, it was a hockey game. I'd like to tell you it was this clearly political moment, but it was never talked about in the locker room. It was never talked about before the game. It was never talked about after the game from a team standpoint. We had great respect for the Soviet players."

Smith asked, "If a kid who's going to the Olympics came up to you and said, 'Should I use this moment to make a political statement?' what would you tell him or her?"

"How strong is it to you? How important is it to you?" Eruzione replied. "Because there [is] going to be some ridicule that you're going to have to face [from] a lot of people. And if you're strong enough to do that, then do it. But I would prefer it not to have it happen. 'Cause it's just going to open up a can of worms for that athlete in whatever situation it is."

And most people agree: according to a new CBS News poll, 82 percent say political expression should *not* have a role at the Olympic Games.

That includes Brian Boitano. Sure, he's in Sochi now to send a message, but at the 1988 Olympics, he kept his issues to himself—on the ice, and on the medal stand.

"You really feel like everyone in America's watching," said Boitano. "You feel like you are America. It's, like, the weirdest feeling in a great way. It's, like, you just feel filled with pride and you just feel like, for that moment, you are America."

## 1968 Olympics

It was, of course, a very different America in 1968.

Dr. Martin Luther King had just been assassinated. Racial tension was at the boiling point.

When there was talk of political demonstrations at the '68 Summer Olympics, International Olympic Committee President Avery Brundage issued a warning: "I don't think any of these boys would be foolish enough to demonstrate at the Olympic Games. And I think if they do they will be promptly sent home."

That year in Mexico City, American sprinters Tommie Smith and John Carlos won the gold and bronze medals, respectively, in the 200 meters.

---

*There are a lot of athletes, prominent athletes, who believe that once you stand up there [on the medal podium], that is not the place to make a political statement.*

---

On the medal stand, they went shoeless as a nod to poverty, wore beads in honor of lynching victims, and as the national anthem played, hung their heads and raised their fists in a salute John Carlos says was not anti-American, but pro-black.

"When we raised our fists, all the people who were loving me yesterday hated me today, merely because I exposed who I was as a black man," said Carlos.

"You could feel it at that moment?" Smith asked.

"At that very same moment."

"You could hear it from the crowd?"

"From the crowd. It wasn't like they were singing the national anthem; it got to the point that they were screaming it, like they were going to shove it down our throats."

Smith and Carlos were thrown off the team and out of the Olympic Village, and flew home to a country that for them would never be the same. At a press conference Carlos said, "There were so many white people telling me that I was a fool and I was standing up on that platform alone."

Smith said, "There are a lot of athletes, prominent athletes, who believe that once you stand up there [on the medal podium], that is not the place to make a political statement."

"Well, maybe they do it in their bedroom. Maybe that's the time and the place," Carlos said. "You know, maybe they go out in Park Avenue, do it out there on Park Avenue. Well, when is the time and the place? To do it when no one can see you? No one can feel you and no one can hear you? No one can try and understand you? Where is the place to do it?

"That's the only place to do it, is where you're going to meet the masses," he said.

"Even if the masses boo you at first?"

"They love me now," Carlos replied.

## After the Olympics

Whatever the outcome of his presence in Sochi, Brian Boitano will come home to multiple projects on and off the ice.

Mike Eruzione of the 1980 hockey team is a motivational speaker with a story no one seems to get tired of hearing.

"We could've lost. And you wouldn't be talking to me," Eruzione laughed.

"Maybe I'd be talking to you for something else," Smith replied.

"Yeah, maybe I'd win the lottery or something."

John Carlos says his actions in Mexico City cost him dearly, and he struggled for years. Today if you visit San Jose State

University, you'll see a statue of Tommie Smith and John Carlos—a tribute to a moment that was, to him, worth any price.

"Yes, I feel that I did the right thing, and God's giving me my rewards for doing it," Carlos told Smith. "Now, I'm not one of the richest guys in the nation, but then again, I don't think that they can buy what I have."

Which is? "My persona. My swagger. My confidence. My faith. And my good looks!"

"You think your Wheaties box is still coming?" asked Smith.

"It might not come in my life and time, but I'd say for people who're just like me, eventually it will be there, where they will come to the realization that we have to start promoting equality and fair play in this society in which we live.

"That sells Wheaties, too."

# 9

# Sex Trafficking Is a Danger at Sporting Events Like the Olympics

*Jeff Sagnip*

*Jeff Sagnip is the press secretary for US Representative Chris Smith, a Republican from New Jersey.*

*Human trafficking, or the transportation of people for the purposes of forced labor or sexual slavery, is a serious problem at sporting events. The Super Bowl attracts traffickers. Russia has a poor record on combating trafficking, which raises concerns about the Sochi Olympic Games. Trafficking can be combated by alerting law enforcement and training transportation personnel to spot trafficking victims and alert the authorities.*

Human trafficking and the Super Bowl, Olympics and other mega sporting venues were the topic of a hearing held Monday by Congressman Chris Smith (NJ-04), Chairman of the House congressional panel that oversees global human rights, and author of the landmark law, the Trafficking Victims Protection Act.

"Lessons Learned from Super Bowl Preparations: Preventing International Human Trafficking at Major Sporting Events," featured the U.S. Dept. of Homeland Security, and airline, train and non-government organization (NGOs) anti-trafficking advocates.

Jeff Sagnip, "Human Trafficking & The Super Bowl," Congtressman Chris Smith, January 27, 2014. www.chrissmith.house.gov. Courtesy of Chris Smith.

## Trafficking and the Super Bowl

"Our hearing focuses on the preparations for the upcoming Super Bowl to prevent human trafficking and strategies employed by airlines, busses and trains, as well as hotels designed to mitigate human trafficking," Smith said. "In less than a week, New Jersey will be hosting the Super Bowl, and along with welcoming enthusiastic fans, the state also is preparing for a likely influx of both domestic and international traffickers. Sadly, but almost certainly, they will bring with them sexually exploited trafficking victims—many of them from abroad—in an attempt to cash in on the Super Bowl crowds. We know from the past, any sports venue—especially the Super Bowl—acts as a sex trafficking magnet."

Smith also spoke of Brazil, host of the 2014 World Cup and the 2016 Summer Olympics, and Russia, host of the 2014 Winter Olympic Games next month. With no formal national procedures to guide Russian law enforcement in the identification of sex trafficking victims Smith is concerned that the 2014 Winter Olympics may turn out to be a "trafficking nightmare." He noted Russia was given the lowest rating by the annual U.S. State Department's Trafficking in Persons Report. In Brazil, despite some improvement in its anti-trafficking laws and taking some steps to mitigate trafficking risks, he said there is much more to do "if they want to protect their children from sex tourism."

*The only standard that fits the crime of human trafficking—zero tolerance—must be rigorously and faithfully enforced by arrests of those engaged in this nefarious trade.*

Worldwide, the best estimates are that as many as 800,000 trafficking victims are moved across international borders every year. Millions more victims are moved within national borders. But anti-trafficking efforts have only recently turned to equipping transportation employees to identify victims in transit. The training is easy, inexpensive, and is already saving lives.

In preparation for the Super Bowl this weekend, the New Jersey Human Trafficking Task Force, which was originally started with seed money from a law Smith authored—the Trafficking Victims Protection Act of 2000—has been working for months to mitigate sex trafficking. It has released anti-trafficking brochures to bus and train employees in New Jersey, as well as reached out to hotels, another major industry on the front lines of spotting traffickers and victims.

## Zero Tolerance

"The only standard that fits the crime of human trafficking—zero tolerance—must be rigorously and faithfully enforced by arrests of those engaged in this nefarious trade—modern-day slavery," Smith said. "And there can be no higher priority than the liberation and protection of the victims. Combating human trafficking must be continuously prioritized at all levels of government, the faith community, civil society and corporations, including the National Football League. All of us must do our part to protect the women and girls."

Maria Odom, Chair of the Blue Campaign at the Department of Homeland Security, testified that victims are often lured with false promises of well-paying jobs or are manipulated by people they trust, and instead are forced or coerced into prostitution, domestic servitude, or types of forced labor. Victims can be any age, citizenship, gender or immigration status, she said.

"Human trafficking is a form of modern-day slavery; a crime that involves the exploitation of someone for the purposes of compelled labor or a commercial sex act through the use of force, fraud, or coercion," Odom said. "Where a person younger than 18 is induced to perform a commercial sex act, it is a crime regardless of whether there is any force, fraud, or coercion. Every year, millions of men, women, and children worldwide—including in the United States—are victims of human trafficking."

## Trafficking in Sochi

Ambassador-at-Large for Trafficking in Persons Luis CdeBaca noted that the upcoming Olympic Winter Games will be hosted in Sochi, Russia. He noted that according to the 2013 Trafficking in Persons Report compiled by the state Department, there "continues to be reports of women and children exploited in sex trafficking in Russia." Major sporting events also require massive capital improvement and infrastructure construction projects, creating a huge demand for cheap labor, he said. At every step of this process, one can see vulnerabilities to human trafficking.

"One of the greatest strengths driving the fight against human trafficking in this country is a government that is galvanized in our commitment: a partnership that has included Congresses and Administrations across the political spectrum for more than a decade," CdeBaca said. "Mr. Chairman, we thank you for this continued, bipartisan success story."

Other witnesses included Polly Hanson, Chief of Police of the National Railroad Passenger Corporation (AMTRAK); Nancy Rivard, President and Founder, Airline Ambassadors International; Carol Smolenski, Executive Director, End Child Prostitution and Trafficking-USA; Letty Ashworth, General Manager of Global Diversity at Delta Airlines; and Holly Smith, a woman who was trafficked as a minor in Atlantic City, N.J. . . .

Holly Smith told the House subcommittee she was a survivor of child sex trafficking within the United States. At age 14 and newly graduated from middle school, she met a man at the local mall who picked her out of the crowd and asked for her phone number. He convinced her to run away from home with him.

"Within hours of running away, though, I was forced into prostitution on the streets and in the casino hotels and motels of Atlantic City, New Jersey," she said. "Thirty-six hours later, I was arrested by police and treated like a criminal. Without appropriate aftercare services, I struggled for many years to overcome my victimization. I struggled with depression, drug abuse, and domestic violence." She survived and rebuilt her life, and today advocates for victims and prevention. . . .

Rivard said Airline Ambassadors worked with Smith to provide a briefing to airlines in 2010 about trafficking, after which American Airlines issued a bulletin to flight personnel and later incorporated the proper reporting protocol into crew manuals.

"As flight attendants, we know that airlines have infrastructure to provide training to flight crew at virtually no cost during annual emergency procedure trainings. Infrastructure is also in place to communicate proper protocol to ground personnel who would be receiving calls from pilots regarding potential trafficking situations," Rivard said.

Ashworth noted that hundreds of thousands of people are trafficked across international borders annually according to the Department of State.

"In addition, sex tourism presents a significant threat as well, with an estimated one million children sexually abused through tourism industries," Ashworth said. "Training employees to spot the indicators of human trafficking, enhancing passenger awareness and coordinating with law enforcement worldwide are essential to combating these threats."

# 10

# Olympic Sex-Trafficking Myth Creates Climate of Fear

*Giedre Steikunaite*

*Giedre Steikunaite is a freelance writer who has worked for the* New Internationalist *and the* Panorama.

*It is widely reported that large sporting events attract traffickers who force women into sexual slavery. However, there is no evidence that trafficking increases around sporting events. The rumors nonetheless result in increased police presence, raids of brothels, and the deportation of immigrant women. Besides these harms, the focus on sporting events distracts attention and resources from the real work of preventing sex trafficking and helping marginalized women. News media should cease reporting irresponsibly on this issue, and authorities should base their policies on facts, not rumors.*

It started with a number. One morning several years ago, Dr Nivedita Prasad from Berlin's Ban Ying Coordination and Counselling Centre against Trafficking in Persons opened a newspaper and panicked: a news report claimed that 40,000 'forced prostitutes' were coming to Germany for the 2006 Football World Cup. 'I thought, where are we going to put 40,000 people?' Prasad recalls. 'There are eight beds in our shelter, and only about 400 in the whole of Berlin!'

She needn't have worried, since it turned out that 40,000 was a fictitious number. What was worrying, however, was the response: 71 police raids in brothels during the football month, compared to 5 to 10 a month in 'normal' times. They resulted in 10 deportations of undocumented (migrant, not trafficked) sex workers. Nobody counted psychological damage.

Such enormous discrepancies between what's predicted and what actually happens have reoccurred during major international sporting events, from the 2004 Olympics in Greece, where no trafficking cases related to the event were found despite fears of 'sex tourism', through Vancouver's 2010 Winter Olympics, the US Super Bowl and the 2010 World Cup in South Africa—where only a tiny increase in paid sex supply was observed.

---

*Given increased police presence during sporting events and the fact that local markets usually meet the demand for paid sex anyway, criminal effort simply wouldn't pay off.*

---

It seems that in the run-up to the 2012 Olympics, London is next in line. On a mission to find trafficked women, intensified police activity—crackdowns on brothels, frequent raids—in the capital's six Olympic boroughs is creating climate of fear among sex workers, says Georgina Perry from Open Doors, an NHS outreach and clinical support for sex workers initiative. Marginalized, sex workers are also cut off from essential health and support services: raids lead to displacement—from a flat to the street—which makes it impossible for health workers to assist them. This crackdown strategy drives business underground, making it more dangerous for women, and they are also less likely to report rape or other forms of violence to the police. 'This is collateral damage of a rumour,' Perry says.

That rumour claims that big sporting events attract multitudes of men who seek paid sex, the increasing demand of which is supposedly met by trafficking. But governmental institution after institution, NGO after NGO, consistently don't find any link between sports events and trafficking for prostitution. South Africa's Department of Justice and Constitutional Development found no cases of trafficking during the 2010 World Cup; five were found in Germany during the 2006 World Cup (less than its monthly average); police didn't notice anything 'out of the ordinary' during recent US Super Bowls. In fact, many sex workers actually take a break during such events. 'I'm going on holiday,' an experienced sex worker told Prasad before the World Cup. 'Business is going to be bad.'

That's because short-term events are not profitable for traffickers, Julie Ham argues in her report 'What's the cost of a rumour?' Given increased police presence during sporting events and the fact that local markets usually meet the demand for paid sex anyway, criminal effort simply wouldn't pay off. But despite all the evidence that there is no evidence, the rumour resurfaces over and over again. Why?

Ironically, it partly comes down to good intentions: media attention provides charities with a good opportunity for more successful fundraising and a good moment to push politicians to 'do something' about trafficking. But more sinister elements are at work, too: moral panic helps justify social control measures such as anti-immigration and anti-prostitution. Portraying women as helpless victims who need to be 'saved' from 'wicked men' upholds common sexist philosophy and maintains hetero-normative attitudes that prevail in our society: surely, the World Cup is a devilish alcohol-and-paid-sex feast for men-turned-beasts, is it not? And the only women present at sporting events are sex workers, right?

This doesn't mean that trafficking should be written off as a problem solved—far from it. To challenge the alleged link between sporting events and trafficking is not to downplay the very serious issue of human trafficking but rather to see the wider picture, says Joanna Busza, senior lecturer in sexual and reproductive health. The worst is that, apart from harassing sex workers, the rumour results in diversion of much needed resources to deal with the real—not imagined—problems: prevention of human trafficking and rights of women as women, as sex workers and as migrants. Anti-trafficking efforts must be 'proportionate, sustainable, evidence-based, cognizant of other sectors in which trafficking occurs, and done in consultation with groups affected by trafficking,' Ham writes in her report. And certainly not only short-term.

Things can be different at London 2012 if priorities are shifted from sensationalism to consistent tackling of the root issues. As Catherine Stephens of the International Union of Sex Workers says, the rumour gets so much media attention because it involves four crucial elements: money, power, gender and sex. Mainstream media knows that all this sells, but remember: it only sells because we buy it.

# 11

# The Special Olympics in LA Will Benefit the City and the Athletes

*Michelle K. Wolf*

*Michelle K. Wolf writes a monthly column for the* Jewish Journal.

*The Special Olympics is an international sports competition for those with developmental disabilities. The 2015 games in Los Angeles offer a chance for the city and the participants to share a message of inspiration and inclusion. The Jewish community of Los Angeles is working to help fund the Israeli Special Olympics delegation, which will join other international delegations in the competition.*

You may not know it, but the world's biggest sports and humanitarian event is coming to Los Angeles this summer [2015], and its impact will be felt locally long after the medals are handed out. In just a few months, the World Games of the Special Olympics will launch at the Los Angeles Memorial Coliseum on July 25, with 7,000 athletes from more than 170 countries, all marching in with their nation's flag for the opening ceremony. The games will continue through Aug. 2.

## The Spirit of Doing Your Best

There will be 25 sports competitions held around Southern California, including at UCLA [University of California, Los Angeles] and USC [University of Southern California], downtown Los Angeles, Long Beach, Griffith Park and the Balboa Sports Complex in Encino. It will also be L.A.'s most widespread public event since the 1984 Olympics. Held every two years, alternating between summer and winter games, the Special Olympics World Games aim to expand the circle of acceptance and inclusion of all people. I had the chance to hear Patrick McClenahan, president and CEO of the 2015 Special Olympics World Games, speak at a recent nonprofit workshop sponsored by Green Hasson Janks, an accounting firm that counts many nonprofits as its clients, among them the *Journal*, as well as the Special Olympics Southern California and the World Games.

---

*The Special Olympics movement has grown to more than 4.4 million athletes around the world, supported by more than 1.3 million coaches and volunteers.*

---

McClenahan, father of an adult daughter with a developmental disability, updated us on the progress of the games and encouraged everyone present to participate as a volunteer and a fan. He said that as great as it is for the Special Olympics athletes to have supportive fans to cheer them on while competing, the fans themselves get even more out of the experience of being there, learning firsthand about "the spirit of doing your best—courage, determination and joy."

To pull off such a massive event at so many venues, the World Games will need 30,000 volunteers and also is recruiting groups of people to sign up ahead of time as "Fans in the Stands." Team captains must be at least 14 years of age and will be responsible for recruiting 10 or more people to come support the athletes during competition. Over the event's nine days, organizers are estimating that 500,000 spectators will turn out. The first Special Olympics World Games were held in 1968 in Chicago, under the leadership of Eunice Kennedy Shriver, sister of President John F. Kennedy, and mother of former first lady of California Maria Shriver and recent L.A. County Supervisor candidate Bobby Shriver. Eunice started the Special Olympics as a summer day camp in the family's backyard in 1962, at a time when children with intellectual disabilities were still routinely placed in state hospitals and other institutions. (Eunice was very close to her sister, Rosemary, who had an intellectual disability made worse after their father, Joe Kennedy, scheduled a lobotomy for her without telling his wife, leaving Rosemary with limited motor and speaking skills.)

Since the first World Games in 1968, the event has grown to be much more than a chance for children and teens with intellectual disabilities to play sports and make friends; the Special Olympics movement has grown to more than 4.4 million athletes around the world, supported by more than 1.3 million coaches and volunteers.

## Helping International Delegations

Along with all the other international delegations coming to participate in the Los Angeles World Games, the games will include 40 Special Olympics athletes from Israel, along with their coaches, doctor and other members of their support team, making a total of 67 in their delegation. The Israeli Special Olympics athletes were selected by a lottery system and will be participating in many different sports, including bowling and kayaking, in which typical athletes play alongside special athletes.

Prior to the games, each country's delegation will be hosted July 21–23 by a Southern California "host town" for recreation, entertainment and cultural events. The Israeli delegation's host town will be Leo Baeck Temple, where one of the congregants, eighth-grader Lucy Meyer, has been a very active part of Special Olympics, and in fact, is a Global Messenger—a Special Olympics athlete now playing a leadership role for the 2015 Special Olympics World Games. Lucy's mother, Jamie, is very enthusiastic about the positive role special Olympics has played in the life of her daughter for many years, and looks forward to sharing that Olympic spirit with the entire Los Angeles Jewish community. There will be more opportunities for community sponsors during the host town period, with details to be finalized soon.

In addition, Susan North Gilboa, the director of the Our-Space Program based at Valley Beth Shalom and Temple Aliyah for members of the Jewish community with special needs and abilities, currently is fundraising to help Team Israel with the costs associated with coming to L.A. The families of the Israeli athletes were asked to raise a total of 320,000 shekels ($85,000) by March 31, and the Special Olympics Israel board is also helping to raise the needed total of $250,000. . . .

There is also a need for home hospitality for family members of the athletes, and L.A. American/Israeli Jewish community members also will be invited especially to cheer during the events in which the Israeli athletes are playing. This will be a win-win experience, no matter who finishes in first place at each event. As the motto for the Special Olympics says, "Let me win. But if I cannot win, let me be brave in the attempt."

# 12

# Rio Will Be Ready for Olympics in 2016

*Associated Press*

*The Associated Press is an international news organization.*

*At first it seemed like Rio de Janeiro might fail to complete preparations for the 2016 Olympics. However, progress has accelerated, and the games seem on track, though some serious problems remain. For example, a subway extension to alleviate traffic is behind schedule, which could result in serious traffic jams. The lagoon around the Olympic park is seriously polluted with sewage, requiring major clean-up. However, such problems should not prevent the Olympics from going forward.*

No one seriously questions any more whether Rio de Janeiro will be ready for the 2016 Olympics.

## Olympics on Track

A year ago, an International Olympic Committee [IOC] vice president called Rio's preparations the "worst" in memory. But since then, work has accelerated as Brazil builds sports arenas, transportation links and hotels.

US network NBC is already airing spots with the headline: "Rio Olympics are coming next summer."

Despite chaotic planning, Brazil pulled off last year's World Cup. Olympic preparations also got off to a troubled start. Despite the progress, deadlines are repeatedly described as "tight" or "tense."

Rio's preparations will come under the spotlight next week, with International Olympic Committee inspectors starting a three-day tour tomorrow (Feb 23 [2015]). IOC President Thomas Bach will also be in town, and the IOC executive board will hold a three-day meeting later in the week.

The political atmosphere has soured since the World Cup. The Brazilian currency has lost 35 per cent of its value against the dollar since Germany won the title seven months ago. President Dilma Rousseff's government has cut services and raised taxes to avoid a revenue shortfall.

---

*Rio is spending about US$14 billion on the Olympics—a mix of public and private money—with the bill expected to rise.*

---

Her popularity has also plunged due to a corruption scandal at state-run oil company Petrobras, where investigators say hundreds of millions have been siphoned off in kickback schemes. Brazil is also facing water and power shortages.

The avalanche of bad news could taint Olympic perceptions, especially if struggling Brazilians blame the two mega-events for the hard times.

Brazil spent about US$12 billion (S$16.3 billion) on the World Cup, most on road and rail projects, and many are still unfinished. Brazil also built at least four football stadiums now viewed as "white elephants."

Rio is spending about US$14 billion on the Olympics—a mix of public and private money—with the bill expected to rise.

Despite the problems, Rio's faults are masked by its image of beaches and party atmosphere, with visitors expecting a good time—no matter what.

Brazilians pride themselves in dreaming up quick solutions to dodge disaster, and pulling off the World Cup shields the Olympics from similar criticism.

"It's always going to be a good asset after everything said about Brazil's World Cup," Mayor Eduardo Paes said last year. "It's always going to be a good excuse for us."

## Ongoing Problems

Far from the television cameras, here are some issues that are sure to come up behind closed doors:

TRAFFIC CHAOS

A 16km subway extension may not be fully operational in time for the games. It's been arduous drilling though a mountain and officials may need a Plan B to get fans from central Rio to the main venue 25km away. Without the subway, vehicles could be wedged into an Olympian traffic jam snaking from Copacabana and Ipanema beaches to the western suburb of Barra da Tijuca, the heart of the games.

NOXIOUS WATERS

Rio state environmental secretary Andre Correa has acknowledged severe pollution in the lagoon that surrounds the Olympic Park and skirts the new golf course. He took a boat ride a few weeks ago through noxious waters, viewing islands of sewage and sludge that appear at low tide. The US$250 million dredging project has been tied up in a dispute. The fetid waters stem from the wealthy and poor alike using the lagoon as a cesspool.

RISING VIOLENCE

Stray bullets injured about 30 people in Rio in January and caused at least five deaths, including a 4-year-old girl and 9-year-old boy. Muggings are also on the rise. The shootouts occur when drug gangs take on each other—or the police. As police have moved in to "pacify" Rio's favelas, gangs have scattered to unpoliced areas. Olympic security could resemble the World Cup: military police, soldiers and lots of hardware.

ROUGH SAILING

The sailing venue in Guanabara Bay is also filthy with untreated waste and floating debris, posing a competitive and health hazard for Olympic sailors. Brazil's most respected health research institute said a few months ago it had detected a drug-resistant super bacteria in the area. Nawal El Moutawakel, the head of the IOC inspection team, said last year: "I don't think we will forgive ourselves if we let the athletes compete in an environment that is not safe and secure."

MAYOR LAWSUIT?

A public prosecutor is looking into a possible lawsuit against Rio Mayor Eduardo Paes alleging improper conduct centering on concessions the city made to a billionaire developer of the new Olympic golf course. The course, which cost about US$20 million to build, has been embroiled in lawsuits over ownership and charges that environmental rules were trampled. The layout will be surrounded by luxury apartments selling in the US$3-8 million range.

# Organizations to Contact

*The editors have compiled the following list of organizations concerned with the issues debated in this book. The descriptions are derived from materials provided by the organizations. All have publications or information available for interested readers. The list was compiled on the date of publication of the present volume; the information provided here may change. Be aware that many organizations take several weeks or longer to respond to inquiries, so allow as much time as possible.*

## Anti-Doping Research, Inc. (ADR)

3873 Grand View Blvd., Los Angeles, CA   90066
(310) 482-6925
e-mail: info@antidopingresearch.org
website: www.antidopingresearch.org

Anti-Doping Research, Inc. (ADR) seeks to rid the sporting world of performance-enhancing drugs by conducting research to find new drugs, identify new ways old substances are being used to enhance performance, and develop new methods of detection. The ADR website provides extensive information about anti-doping tactics with an anti-doping timeline, educational videos, and access to a range of publications dealing with steroids and other topics.

## The Brookings Institution

1775 Massachusetts Ave. NW, Washington, DC   20036
(202) 797-6000 • fax: (202) 797-6004
e-mail: communications@brookings.edu
website: www.brookings.edu

The Brookings Institution is a private nonprofit organization devoted to conducting independent research and developing innovative policy solutions. Brookings' goal is to provide high-quality analysis and recommendations for decision makers on the full range of challenges facing an increasingly interdependent world. The Brookings Institution publishes numerous policy papers and reports available at their website, including articles on the international policy ramifications of the Olympics.

## Canadian Olympic Committee

21 St. Clair Ave., E., Suite 900, Toronto, ON   M4T 1L9
 Canada
(416) 962-0262 • fax: (416) 967-4902
e-mail: digital@olympic.ca
website: www.olympic.ca

The Canadian Olympic Committee is a privately funded, non-profit organization that supports the Canadian Olympic team. The group's website includes news items, profiles of athletes and sports, and other articles.

## Cato Institute

1000 Massachusetts Ave. NW, Washington, DC   20001-5403
(202) 842-0200 • fax: (202) 842-3490
website: www.cato.org

The Cato Institute conducts research on public policy issues in order to promote consideration of traditional American principles of limited government, individual liberty, free markets, and peace. It publishes reviews and journals such as *Economic Freedom of the World* and *Cato Journal*, as well as policy papers and opinion pieces on economic and other issues. It has many policy articles on the economics and politics of the Olympic Games.

## International Olympic Committee (IOC)

Chateau de Vidy, Lausanne   CH-1007
 Switzerland
website: www.olympic.org

The International Olympic Committee (IOC) oversees the Olympic Games. It determines which cities will host the games and sets policies on drug use and on transgendered and disabled athletes. The website includes articles on events, athletes, countries, and more. The site includes the Olympic Studies Centre, which promotes academic research on the Olympic Games.

### International Paralympic Committee (IPC)

Adenaureallee 212-214, Bonn   53113
  Germany
e-mail: info@paralympic.org
website: www.paralympic.org

The International Paralympic Committee (IPC) is an umbrella organization that oversees athletes with all types of disabilities in several sports. It holds and oversees the Paralympic Games, an international sporting competition that is parallel to the Olympic Games. Its website includes news updates, articles on sports and athletes, and digital issues of the IPC's monthly magazine, *The Paralympian.*

### Special Olympics

1133 19th St. NW, Washington, DC   20036-3604
(202) 628-3630 • fax: (202) 824-0200
e-mail: info@specialolympics.org
website: www.specialolympics.org

The Special Olympics is a global sports organization for children and adults with mental and developmental disabilities. The organization holds local competitions as well as the summer and winter Special Olympics World Games. The Special Olympics website includes information on athletes, events, and sports competitions.

### United States Olympic Committee (USOC)

One Olympic Plaza, Colorado Springs, CO   80909
(719) 632-5551
website: www.teamusa.org

The United States Olympic Committee (USOC) is a nonprofit private organization that coordinates all Olympic-related activity in the United States. It works with the International

Olympic Committee and other organizations to discourage the use of steroids and other drugs in sports. Information on USOC programs can be found at the Committee's website.

## US Anti-Doping Agency (USADA)
5555 Tech Center Drive, Suite 200
Colorado Springs, CO   80919-2372
(719) 785-2900 • fax: (719) 785-2001
website: www.usada.org

The US Anti-Doping Agency (USADA) serves as the United States Olympic movement's anti-doping organization. In order to preserve the integrity of competition, the agency works to deter athletes from engaging in illicit substance use, implements a sanctions program that punishes those athletes who seek to gain a competitive edge through the use of performance-enhancing substances, and engages in cutting-edge research to ensure the most comprehensive and up-to-date methods of doping control. Detailed information about banned and allowed substances can be found at the USADA website along with information about drug testing carried out by the agency. The biannual *Spirit of Sport* newsletter can be read online as well.

## World Anti-Doping Agency (WADA)
Stock Exchange Tower, 800 Place Victoria, Suite 1700
Montreal, Quebec   H4Z 1B7
   Canada
(514) 904-9232 • fax: (514) 904-8650
e-mail: info@wada-ama.org
website: www.wada-ama.org

The World Anti-Doping Agency (WADA) has been working since its founding in 1999 to achieve an international doping-free sporting environment through a combination of scientific research, education campaigns, development of anti-doping techniques, and observation of the World Anti-Doping Code. The WADA website offers detailed information about the World Anti-Doping Program, the Anti-Doping Community, and the organization's research. Further details about the association's education and awareness programs directed at youth can be found online as well.

# Bibliography

## Books

Stephen Frawley and Darryl Adair, eds.  *Managing the Olympics.* New York: Palgrave Macmillan, 2013.

Keith Gilber and Otto J. Schantz  *The Paralympic Games: Empowerment or Side Show?* Indianapolis, IN: Cardinal Publisher's Group, 2009.

Vassil Girginov  *The Olympics: A Critical Reader.* London: Routledge, 2010.

Douglas Hartmann  *Race, Culture, and the Revolt of the Black Athlete: The 1968 Olympic Protests and Their Aftermath.* Chicago: University of Chicago Press, 2004.

David Hassan, Sandra Dowling, and Roy McConkey, eds.  *Sport, Coaching and Intellectual Disability.* London: Routledge, 2014.

Graeme Hayes and John Karamichas, eds.  *Olympic Games, Mega-Events and Civil Societies: Globalization, Environment, Resistance.* New York: Palgrave Macmillan, 2012.

Thomas M. Hunt  *Drug Games: The International Olympic Committee and the Politics of Doping, 1960–2008.* Austin: University of Texas Press, 2011.

Arnd Kruger and William Murray, eds.
*The Nazi Olympics: Sport, Politics, and Appeasement in the 1930s.* Champaign: University of Illinois Press, 2003.

Iain Lindsay
*Living with London's Olympics: An Ethnography.* New York: Palgrave Macmillan, 2014.

David Miller
*The Official History of the Olympic Games and the IOC: Athens to London 1894–2012.* New York: Mainstream Publishing, 2012.

Bo Petersson and Karina Vamiling, eds.
*The Sochi Predicament: Contexts, Characteristics and Challenges of the Olympic Winter Games in 2014.* Cambridge, UK: Cambridge Scholars Publishing, 2013.

Holger Preuss
*The Economics of Staging the Olympics: A Comparison of the Games, 1972–2008.* Cheltenham, UK: Edward Elgar Publishing, 2006.

Steven Ungerleider
*Faust's Gold: Inside the East German Doping Machine.* New York: Thomas Dunne Books, 2015.

Andrew Zimbalist
*Circus Maximus: The Economic Gamble Behind Hosting the Olympics and the World Cup.* Washington, DC: Brookings Institution Press, 2015.

David Zirin
*Brazil's Dance with the Devil: The World Cup, the Olympics, and the Struggle for Democracy.* Chicago: Haymarket Books, 2014.

## Periodicals and Internet Sources

Lindsay Abrams          "Sochi's Bleak Future: What Happens to Olympic Cities After the Olympics Are Over?," *Salon*, February 23, 2014. www.salon.com.

Mark Arsenault          "Boston Olympics Would Bring Billions, Study Says," *Boston Globe*, March 18, 2015.

Liz Clarke              "Sochi Olympics Played Differently to Different Audiences," *Washington Post*, February 22, 2014.

Daphnee Denis           "Scrap the Paralympics," *Slate*, August 9, 2012. www.slate.com.

Fred Dews               "Sochi Olympics a Big Success for Putin and Russia," Brookings Institution, February 24, 2014. www.brookings.edu.

*Economist*             "Protest in China: Post-Olympic Stress Disorder," September 11, 2008.

*Economist*             "Sporting Mega-Events: Just Say No," February 28, 2015.

Josh Eidelson           "Most Corrupt Olympics Ever: Why Sochi's 'Above and Beyond' What We've Seen Before," *Salon*, February 7, 2014. www.salon.com.

Richard Florida         "Never Host a Mega-Event?," *Citylab*, January 29, 2014. www.citylab.com.

Mobina Jaffer | "What Human Trafficking Has to Do with the Olympics," *Huffington Post*, July 27, 2012. www.huffingtonpost.com.

Ian Johnson | "Scientists Question Environmental Impact of China's Winter Olympics Bid," *New York Times*, April 9, 2015.

Jeré Longman | "Pursuing Games, Boston Jumps In with One Foot," *New York Times*, January 9, 2015.

Ben Mathis-Lilley | "IOC Reforms Would Allow Multiple Countries to Co-Host Olympics," *Slate*, December 8, 2014. www.slate.com.

Julie Mollins | "Q+A-London Olympics: The Sex-Trafficking Event That Wasn't," Thomson Reuters Foundation, November 28, 2012. www.trust.org.

Dom Phillips | "Polluted Waters Could Force Rio de Janeiro to Move 2016 Olympic Races," *Washington Post*, May 15, 2015.

Elizabeth Plank | "Want to Stand with Gay Athletes? Then Don't Boycott the Sochi Olympics," *PolicyMic*, August 8, 2013. www.mic.com.

Patrick Rishe | "Boston 2024: Did USOC Make the Right Olympic Choice?," *Forbes*, January 12, 2015.

Amanda Terkel  "Athletes Pressure Olympics to Take a Stand on Kazakhstan's Anti-Gay Legislation," *Huffington Post*, May 15, 2015. www.huffingtonpost.com.

Jeff Thomson  "Mind the Accounting Talent Gap: Q-and-A with Former Special Olympics CFO," *Forbes*, April 15, 2013.

Pang Zhongying  "The Beijing Olympics and China's Soft Power," Brookings Institution, September 4, 2008. www.brookings.edu.

# Index

CPSIA information can be obtained
at www.ICGtesting.com
Printed in the USA
FFOW05n0835120116